Pebble™ Plus

Under the Sea
Sea Turtles

by Carol K. Lindeen

Consulting Editor: Gail Saunders-Smith, PhD
Consultant: Jody Rake, Member
Southwest Marine/Aquatic Educator's Association

Capstone
press
Mankato, Minnesota

Pebble Plus is published by Capstone Press,
151 Good Counsel Drive, P.O. Box 669, Mankato, Minnesota 56002.
www.capstonepress.com

1 2 3 4 5 6 09 08 07 06 05 04

Library of Congress Cataloging-in-Publication Data
Lindeen, Carol K., 1976–
    Sea turtles / by Carol K. Lindeen.
    p. cm.—(Pebble Plus: Under the sea)
    Includes bibliographical references (p. 23) and index.
    ISBN 0-7368-2601-7 (hardcover)
    ISBN 0-7368-5113-5 (paperback)
    1. Sea turtles—Juvenile literature. [1. Sea turtles. 2. Turtles.] I. Title. II. Series.
QL666.C536L56 2005
597.92'8—dc22   2003025611

Summary: Simple text and photographs present the lives of sea turtles.

Editorial Credits
Martha E. H. Rustad, editor; Juliette Peters, designer; Kelly Garvin, photo researcher;
    Karen Hieb, product planning editor

Photo Credits
DigitalVision/Stephen Frink, 1
Michael Patrick O'Neill, 8–9
Minden Pictures/Birgitte Willms, cover; Mike Parry, 16–17, 18–19
PhotoDisc Inc., back cover
Seapics.com/David B. Fleetham, 4–5, 20–21; Doug Perrine, 6–7, 10–11; James D. Watt, 12–13, 14–15

Note to Parents and Teachers

The Under the Sea series supports national science standards related to the diversity
and unity of life. This book describes and illustrates sea turtles. The images support
early readers in understanding the text. The repetition of words and phrases helps early
readers learn new words. This book also introduces early readers to subject-specific
vocabulary words, which are defined in the Glossary section. Early readers may need
assistance to read some words and to use the Table of Contents, Glossary, Read More,
Internet Sites, and Index/Word List sections of the book.

Word Count: 118
Early-Intervention Level: 14

Table of Contents

Sea Turtles

What are sea turtles?

Sea turtles are reptiles.

Sea turtles poke their beaks
out of the water to breathe.

Sea turtles swim and crawl with their flippers. Hard shells protect the soft bodies of sea turtles.

Sea turtles are about
as long as a child is tall.
Some grow to be as long
as a tall adult.

Migrating

Some sea turtles migrate.
They swim far to find
food and mates.

Sea turtles find currents of
warm water. The currents
help sea turtles swim
long distances quickly.

Female sea turtles crawl
on beaches. They dig
holes and lay their eggs.

Young sea turtles hatch on beaches. They hurry to the sea to find safety.

Under the Sea

Sea turtles swim
under the sea.

Glossary

beak—a hard mouthpart on some animals; turtles have beaks instead of teeth.

current—moving water that flows faster than the rest of the water

flipper—a flat limb with bones on the bodies of some sea animals; flippers help turtles swim in water and move on land.

mate—an animal that joins with another animal to produce young

migrate—to travel from one area to another on a regular basis

reptile—a cold-blooded animal that breathes air and has a backbone; most reptiles lay eggs and have scaly skin.

shell—a hard covering on the outside of some animals

Read More

Cerullo, Mary M. *Sea Turtles: Ocean Nomads.* New York: Dutton's Children's Books, 2003.

Laskey, Elizabeth. *Sea Turtles.* Sea Creatures. Chicago: Heinemann Library, 2003.

Rustad, Martha E. H. *Sea Turtles.* Ocean Life. Mankato, Minn.: Pebble Books, 2001.

Internet Sites

FactHound offers a safe, fun way to find Internet sites related to this book. All of the sites on FactHound have been researched by our staff.

Here's how:

1. Visit *www.facthound.com*

2. Type in this special code **0736826017** for age-appropriate sites. Or enter a search word related to this book for a more general search.

3. Click on the **Fetch It** button.

FactHound will fetch the best sites for you!

Index/Word List